An Intimate Note
to the Sincere Seeker

Also by Sri Sri Ravi Shankar

Wisdom for the New Millennium

God Loves Fun

Celebrating Silence
— highlights from An Intimate Note
to the Sincere Seeker, Vols. 1–5

A Gift of Silence: Guided Meditations by Sri Sri (CD)

Waves of Beauty

Bang on the Door

TALKS PUBLISHED SINGLY:

The Language of the Heart

Prayer, the Call of the Soul

The Way Back Home

For a complete catalog, contact
VYAKTI VIKAS KENDRA
Tel. 91-80-6645106
email: vvkpress@vsnl.com
Outside India, see back pages.

An Intimate Note to the Sincere Seeker

Volume 7: July 12, 2001 – July 11, 2002

weekly knowledge from

Sri Sri Ravi Shankar

compiled by Bill Hayden & Anne Elixhauser

VYAKTI VIKAS KENDRA

Published by
VYAKTI VIKAS KENDRA, INDIA
No. 19, 39th A Cross, 11th Main
IV T Block, Jayanagar
Bangalore 560 041
email: vvkpress@vsnl.com

Compiled by Bill Hayden and Anne Elixhauser
Cover and interior design: Jeffrey Ainis
Editorial review: Laura Weinberg and Jeffrey Ainis

Printed in India
by Elegant Printing Works, Bangalore
80-6615507

ISBN 1-885289-41-3
First Edition

Let the wind that blows be sweet
Let the oceans flow honey
Let all the herbs and plant kingdom be favorable to us
Let the nights be sweet and let the days be sweet
Let the dust of this planet be sweet to us
Let the heavens and our forefathers be sweet to us
Let all the trees be laden with honey
Let the sun be sweet to us
and let all the radiations be favorable to us
Let all the animals be sweet to us
Let our food be favorable to us
Let all our thoughts and our speech
be sweet like honey.

Let our life be pure and divine,
Let it be sweet like honey.

— Sri Sri Ravi Shankar

Introduction

In June of 1995, Sri Sri Ravi Shankar began a weekly
tradition of creating a short talk on a subject relevant
to current events or to the collective minds of those
who walked his path. The current Weekly Knowledge
— as these notes from Sri Sri have come to be
called — applies to an immediate issue or need, but
there have been many instances where someone seeking
wisdom or advice randomly opened a volume to find
exactly what was needed at that moment. The paradigm
of individual minds, separated by time and space, breaks
down. Those sincerely seeking guidance and life's truths
will find these to be timeless touchstones.

Those fortunate enough to be with Sri Sri when
this knowledge is created, find that the discussion
draws wisdom from Sri Sri that satisfies the heart and
enriches the intellect. It is always intimate, lively,
extemporaneous, brilliant and often humorous. In the
words of Sri Sri, "Being with the guru means spontaneous integration of life and wisdom."

Included with each Weekly Knowledge message is
a News Flash that documents the journey that this
remarkable man takes around the world and through
people's hearts and lives. In the News Flash, Sri Sri is
called Guruji, the name many use for him out of
respect and love.

These intimate notes to sincere seekers have been
collected each year into volumes and made available to
the world.

The journey for this collection begins at the Guru
Purnima Course on July 12, 2001, at Lake Tahoe,
California, United States, and ends on July 11, 2002,
at an undisclosed location – a rare occurrence but perhaps an opportunity for a private meeting or a time to
rest and plan.

Sri Sri Ravi Shankar

Contents

Mistakes /19

The Great Pleasure
  of Rest /21

Worry & Feelings /23

Who is Pleasing Whom? /25

Two Perspectives of
  the Guru /27

Love & Authority /29

Ganesha /31

Hungry for Power /33

You & Ownership /35

Reverence & Ownership /37

War: the Worst Act
  of Reason /39

Terrorism: the Cause
  & the Remedy /43

How to Deal
  With Anxiety /47

Is War Violence or
  Non-violence? /49

Honey /51

Drop Your Intentions /53

Aishwarya & Madhurya /55

Volunteer /57

Adulation /61

Seva /63

Confidence With Humility:
  the Rarest Combination /65

Dreaming the Impossible /67

Respect & Ego /69

Maya /71

Letting Go of Control /73

Memory: a Hindrance
  & a Blessing /75

Don't be Perturbed
  by Foolishness /77

Glory & Dispassion
  (Vaibhav & Vairagya) /79

Where Dispassion
  is Detrimental! /81

Business & Spirituality /83

The Subtle Truth
About Virtues /85

Humor & Humiliation /87

Love & Truth /91

An Awkward Situation /93

The True Yajña /97

Your Nature is Shiva /99

Praise the Fools /101

What Makes a
Real Holiday /103

Wake Up & Slow Down /105

Communism
& Spirituality /107

Was Buddha an Atheist? /109

The Strength of
Commitment /111

Two Types of
Knowledge /113

Friendship for a Cause / 115

Three Types
of Dispassion / 117

Faith & Alertness /119

Enthusiasm
& Dispassion /121

Guru Tidbits /123

Nigraha, Agraha, Satyagraha
& Duraagraha /125

Wake Up & Transcend /127

Art of Living Foundation
Programs & Courses /129

Art of Living Bookstore /135

Worldwide Art of Living
Centers /137

An Intimate Note
to the Sincere Seeker

Mistakes

Mistakes happen all the time. You often get irritated by mistakes and you want to correct them, but how many can you correct? You correct others' mistakes for two reasons. First is when someone's mistake bothers you, and second is when you correct someone for their sake so that they can grow, not because it bothers you. Correcting mistakes in the first case, when the mistake bothers you, does not work.

To correct mistakes you need both authority and love. Authority and love seem to be contradictory but in reality they are not. Authority without love is stifling and does not work. Love without authority is shallow. You need both but they need to be in the right combination so that you can be successful in correcting others' mistakes. This can happen if you are totally dispassionate and centered.

When you allow room for mistakes, you can be both authoritative and sweet. That is how the Divine is — the right balance of both. Krishna and Jesus had both. People in love also exercise authority with those they love. Authority and love exist in all relationships.

ABHAY: The husband just loves and the wife has the authority.

MIKEY: Is that a mistake?

SRI SRI: I don't want to correct it! (laughter)

Jai Guru Dev
Lake Tahoe, California
United States

News Flash

Guruji was resplendent rafting down the river, with all the course participants following and chanting bhajans.

The Great Pleasure of Rest

There is pleasure in rest and pleasure in activity.
The pleasure in activity is momentary and causes
fatigue, while the pleasure in rest is magnanimous and
energizing. So to the one who has tasted pleasure in
rest (samadhi), the pleasure in activity is insignificant.
All activities that you do, you do so that you can have
deep rest. Activity is part of the system. However, the
real pleasure is in samadhi. In order to have deep rest
one must be active. The proper balance of both is
essential.

Many seek pleasure in this or that, but the wise
man just smiles. The real rest is only in knowledge.

Jai Guru Dev
North American Ashram, Quebec
Canada

News Flash
*At 46,000 feet, on the flight from Lake Tahoe to Montreal,
2+1 really did become 0! After 11-1/2 years, the beautiful "I
don't know" became a reality, with numerous devotees finally*

getting it. If you "don't know" what this means, listen to *Bhakti Sutras* Tape 12.

Preparation for the yajñas is already underway. Nine pundits from India have arrived at the North American Ashram to begin the yajñas, which are ancient ceremonies for creating beneficial effects in the environment.

Worry & Feelings

The head worries and the heart feels. The two cannot function at the same time. When your feelings dominate, worry dissolves.

If you worry a lot, your feelings are dead and you are stuck in your head. Worrying makes your mind and heart inert and dull. It steals your energy and prevents you from thinking clearly. Worries are like a rock in the head. They entangle you; they trap you in a cage. Worries are uncertain since they are about the future.

When you feel, you do not worry. Feelings are like flowers, they come up, they blossom and they die. Feelings rise, they fall and then disappear. When your feelings are expressed, you feel relieved. When you are angry, you express your anger and the next moment you feel fine. Or when you are upset, you cry and you get over it. Feelings last for some short time and then they drop away, but worry eats at you for longer periods of time and eventually consumes you.

Feelings make you spontaneous. Children feel so they are spontaneous, but adults put brakes on their feelings and start worrying. Worry obstructs action while feelings propel action. Worrying about negative feelings is a blessing because it puts brakes on those feelings, preventing you from acting on them. Worries about positive feelings usually never occur. Often you start worrying about your feelings when you think you are feeling too much.

Offering your worries is prayer and prayer moves you in feelings.

Jai Guru Dev
North American Ashram, Quebec
Canada

Who is Pleasing Whom?

God created man and the whole world with so many varieties, so many good things. God made so many types of vegetables, fragrances, flowers and thorns, dragons and horrors, to please man and keep him entertained. But man became more and more depressed.

God then acted tough and man had to start pleasing Him. So man kept himself busy pleasing God and he became happier since he had no time to get worried or depressed. When you have someone to please, it keeps you on your toes and you are happier. But if your goal is just to please yourself, depression is sure to follow.

Pleasure simply brings more craving. But the problem is that we try to get contentment through pleasure. True contentment can only come through service.

Jai Guru Dev
European Ashram, Bad Antogast
Germany

News Flash

People from 29 countries are gathered in the European Ashram for an enlightening Advanced Course.

Two Perspectives of the Guru

In the Orient, having a master is considered a matter of pride. A master is a symbol of security, love and a sign of great wealth. Being with a guru is like being with one's higher self. Not having a master was looked down upon as being an orphan or poor, or a sign of misfortune. Those without a master were considered to be orphans, but not those without parents. But in the Occident having a master is considered a matter of shame and a sign of weakness, for there masters are known for enslaving people.

In the Orient people take pride in having a guru for every discipline — a religious guru (dharmaguru), a family guru (kulaguru), a guru for the kingdom (raj-guru), a guru for a particular discipline (vidyaguru), and a spiritual guru (sadguru).

In the Orient, masters make their disciples feel powerful, while in the Occident, masters are thought to make people weak. In the Orient, there is a deep sense of belongingness that enables people to dissolve their limited identity into infinity. But in the Occident, a master is considered to be a motivator and one who provokes competition.

Jai Guru Dev
European Ashram, Bad Antogast
Germany

News Flash

The social welfare minister, Shiv Kumar, inaugurated the Institute for Rural Development in Bangalore.

Art of Living leaders are leading U.N. conferences in Geneva this week.

Bad Antogast is overflowing with various courses. Preparations for yajñas are on at the European Ashram.

Love & Authority

Love and authority are totally opposite values yet they co-exist.

The grosser the consciousness, the more pronounced the authority must be. The more refined and subtle the consciousness, the less need there is to exercise authority.

When you are unrefined, you demand authority and when you demand authority, love recedes. Asserting authority indicates lack of confidence and love. The more evident one's authority, the less sensitive and effective it will be.

A sensible person will not demand authority at all but will assume it. The most effective CEO's will not make you feel their authority, for authority can never bring inspiration.

Your sincere servant has more authority over you than your boss, isn't that so? A baby has full authority over his mother. Similarly, a devotee has complete authority over the Divine, though he never exercises it.

The subtler you become, the more authority you gain. The greater the love, the subtler will be the authority. The lesser the love, the more pronounced will be the authority.

Jai Guru Dev
Bangalore Ashram
India

News Flash

Yajñas were performed for world peace in the European Ashram, and Krishna's birthday was celebrated with gaiety.

The Bangalore Ashram is buzzing with blissful faces as Guruji arrives for his hectic program.

Ganesha

The lord of the diverse universe is called Ganesha.

The whole universe is nothing but groups of atoms, groups of qualities, of energy. *Gana* means group and a group cannot exist without a lord. Like the queen bee, whose mere existence brings forth the honeycomb, this diverse universe in itself is enough evidence for Ganesha's presence.

Ganesha, or Lord, was born from the unmanifest transcendental consciousness, the Self, called Shiva. Just as when atoms bond, matter comes into existence; so when all the fragmented aspects of human consciousness bond, Divinity happens effortlessly and that is the birth of Ganesha from Shiva.

Jai Guru Dev
Bangalore Ashram
India

News Flash
The Ganesha Festival was celebrated in the Bangalore Ashram. The Ashram school has been accredited as the best school in Bangalore because for the third time in a row the

school students achieved 100% on their test results. Being a first generation school (i.e. the children are the first generation in their families to get an education) this feat is truly remarkable!

This week 2,400 prison inmates in the Tihar Jail, New Delhi, are taking the Art of Living Course. This is the largest ever Art of Living Course, requiring 20 teachers.

Recent research conducted by Dr. H. Geetha, professor of biochemistry at the Bangalore Medical College, shows a marked improvement in cholesterol levels after practicing Sudarshan Kriya.

Weekly Knowledge No. 320
August 30, 2001

Hungry for Power

Why are people hungry for power?

People are hungry for power because they want attention and recognition. Power is a means, just like money. Passion is for an end. People who do not see power or money as a means but as an end in itself do not live, they simply exist. If you do not realize that you are THE power, that you are enlightened, then you crave for power.

You crave for attention and recognition if you do not have any talents, love or passion, or if you are not innocent and childlike.

If you do not have any talents and you are not contributing anything substantial to society, like an artist, a scientist, an Art of Living teacher or a volunteer, then you are hungry for power.

If you do not have a love or a passion to bring about a transformation in society, then you are hungry for power.

If you are not innocent and childlike and do not have a sense of belongingness with the whole world, then you are hungry for power.

Those who do not have any of these four, like some politicians, also crave for power.

True power is the power of the spirit; real confidence, strength and happiness all spring from the spirit. And one who knows this and has this is not hungry at all for power.

Jai Guru Dev
Bangalore Ashram
India

News Flash

Kerala Day, the Onam Festival, was celebrated in the Bangalore Ashram.

Art of Living members are leading the Educational Caucus and the Spirituality and Religion Caucus at the U.N. conference in Durban.

You & Ownership

Man has a tendency to own things. When he owns something small his mind stays small, his life gets stifled and his whole consciousness is immersed in his house, car, spouse, children and such. A recluse leaves his home and goes far away. There also he starts owning his asana, rosary, books, concepts and his knowledge.

Owning has simply shifted from objects and people to ideas and practices. But a wise one knows that he owns the sun, the moon, the stars, the air, all of space and the Divine in its entirety. When you own something big then your consciousness also expands, and when you own something small then small negative emotions start coming up, such as anger and greed.

I wonder why people do not feel connected to the sun? The very existence of life depends upon the sun. Perhaps it is lack of awareness that causes people to refuse to acknowledge and own their connectedness to the macrocosmic universe. The rishis in ancient India, the Native Americans and the aboriginals from all over the globe have insisted that you can feel connected to the sun, the moon and the directions.

When you own something magnanimous your consciousness also becomes magnanimous.

Jai Guru Dev
Bangalore Ashram
India

News Flash

Thousands of people arrived from Kerala to celebrate the festival of Onam in the Bangalore Ashram. A big feast was served for the celebration.

Dean and Shirley Harmison, Werner Luedemann and the entire South African team participated in the Durban U.N. Conference on Racism. The Art of Living provided the chairperson for leading the conference and for the educator caucus.

The U.K. and U.S.A. teams of musicians are taking the college students in Bangalore, Chennai, Vizag and Kolkata by storm. The West Zone Teacher's Meet in the Bangalore Ashram was simply stupendous. The teachers left with more zeal and enthusiasm.

There was a rousing welcome for Guruji in Pune.

Weekly Knowledge No. 322
September 24, 2001

Reverence & Ownership

Often you do not have reverence for that which you own, and losing that reverence happens unconsciously.

Whatever you revere becomes bigger than you. When you have reverence in all your relationships then your own consciousness expands. Then even small things appear to be significant and big. Every little creature appears to be dignified. It is the reverence in every relationship that saves the relationship.

When you have reverence for the whole universe, you are in harmony with the whole universe. Then you do not need to reject or renounce anything.

Reverence in ownership frees you from greed, jealousy and lust. Cultivate the skill of having reverence every moment in your life.

Jai Guru Dev
Bangalore Ashram
India

News Flash

En route to Himachal Pradesh, the hill state of India, Guruji had a lively satsang in Delhi. Guruji was given a red-carpet welcome at Kalka as a State Guest of Himachal Pradesh. After brief satsangs in Purwanoo and Solan, Guruji arrived at Simla, a famous hill station, where he received a moving traditional welcome with horns, music and dances. At Simla, Guruji addressed the senior bureaucrats of the State Government at the State Guest House. A MahaKriya and a big satsang attended by thousands were held the following day.

On to Uttar Pradesh, the largest state of India, where Guruji was again invited as a State Guest to the state capital, Lucknow. He was received there by an enthusiastic crowd of several thousand people. His address to the prominent people of Lucknow was laced with wit and humor. Guruji gifted cycles, wheelchairs and hearing aids to 500 physically challenged. Several thousand were blissed out in the evening satsang.

Guruji returned to Delhi for yet another blissful satsang with thousands of devotees. Also on the agenda was an inspiring address to over 5,000 village youth at a conference attended by Uma Bharati, Minister for Youth in India.

It was a whirlwind tour, and it was as if an Art of Living wave swept across all the cities that Guruji visited.

War: the Worst Act of Reason

The worst act of reason is war.

Every war has a reason, and the reason justifies the war. Those who engage in war reason it out. But reason is limited. As reason changes, the justification falls apart. All the reasons for every war appear to be justifiable to some limited minds and for a limited time. Hence, war becomes inevitable on this planet.

War is limited to human beings. No other species in creation engages in war or mass destruction, as they have no reason. Animals have their prey and let everything just be. But mankind, from time immemorial, has engaged in war because man lives on reason. Man gives reason to every act of his and justifies it. As reasons change, his justifications fall apart.

Man has to transcend reason, and only then can he realize Divinity. Then he will not engage in war. Only when people become sensible, rise above hatred and have heightened consciousness can war be stopped.

Jai Guru Dev
Kolkata
India

News Flash

Guruji arrived in Shillong to a tumultuous welcome by the Governor and the Chief Minister. For the first time ever Shillong had huge gatherings as thousands were rapt in meditation and high in spirit during satsang.

Guruji was the state guest of four different Indian states — Meghalaya, Assam, West Bengal and Tripura! Estimated crowds of over 250,000 people came for darshan and blessings from Guruji, and over 35,000 people did Sudarshan Kriya with Guruji!

At Kolkata, Guruji and His Holiness the Dalai Lama addressed delegates of the Kolkata Chamber of Commerce. The evening satsang had 30,000 people rapt in meditation and blissfully singing bhajans. Memorable yajñas were performed at Kolkata and Guwahati for harmony in the world. Guwahati welcomed Guruji with beautiful tribal folk songs and dances. Guruji emphasized the need to protect the rich and diverse tribal culture. Thousands braved the rains to be in the evening satsang. Guruji inaugurated the Sri Sri Ravi Shankar Vidya Mandir (school) in Guwahati by ringing a bell. After a cruise on the river Brahmaputra, the entourage left for Siliguri for a stay of less than 24 hours.

Siliguri, a town in the foothills of Darjeeling, celebrated his arrival with all roads leading to the mega satsang. Guruji's entourage had no risk of getting lost, as any resident of the town could guide them to Guruji's residence and the satsang. Thousands attended the morning MahaKriya where they did Sudarshan Kriya with Guruji, and over 50,000 people were singing, dancing and celebrating the grace of Guruji at the mega satsang. Guruji graced the Sri Sri Ravi Shankar Vidya Mandir and inaugurated the Rural Training Centre in the Siliguri Ashram. The entourage then headed to Agartala for the last leg of Guruji's tour of India's northeast.

Terrorism: the Cause & the Remedy

The act which is only destructive and inflicts suffering on both oneself and others, is terrorism. In such an act human values are lost in the process of achieving a goal.

Some of the factors that lead to terrorism are:

- Frustration and desperation in achieving a goal
- Confused emotions
- Shortsightedness and impulsive action
- Belief in a non-verifiable concept of heaven and merit; a childish concept of God where God favors some and is angry with others, undermining the omniscience and omnipotence of the Divine.

Terrorism induces fear psychosis in everyone, increases poverty, suffering and loss of life with no apparent gain. Instead of life-supporting solutions the terrorist chooses destruction as an answer. If you criticize without giving a solution, know that it comes from the seed of terrorism.

Although there are certain qualities you can appreciate in a terrorist such as fearlessness, commitment to a goal, and sacrifice, you must learn from them things that you should never do. These are valuing some ideas and concepts more than life, having a narrow perspective of life, and dishonoring its diversity.

The remedy for terrorism is:

- Inculcating a broader perspective of life.
- Valuing life more than race, religion and nationality.
- Providing education in human values — friendliness, compassion, cooperation and upliftment.
- Teaching methods to release stress and tension.
- Cultivating confidence in achieving noble aims by peaceful and non-violent means.
- Weeding out destructive tendencies with spiritual upliftment.

QUESTION: Can terrorism be more than physical violence, such as cultural or economic violence?

SRI SRI: Yes. The solution for economic violence is to "Think globally, buy locally," and the solution for cultural violence is to "Broaden your vision, deepen your roots."

QUESTION: How does one cope with the aftermath of terrorism?

SRI SRI: Faith and prayer. When disaster happens, anger is inevitable. To take precautions that one does not react improperly, wisdom is needed not emotional outbursts. One mistake cannot be corrected by another mistake. Strive to have multicul-

tural and multireligious education and have spiritual
upliftment reach every part of the globe, for the
world will not be safe if even a small pocket of people are left ignorant.

Jai Guru Dev
European Ashram, Bad Antogast
Germany

News Flash

*A record crowd, the likes of which has never before been seen
in the state, listened in rapt attention to Guruji at the satsang
in Tripura, a state in the remote northeastern region of India.
Our school was opened in a part of the royal palace in
Agartala — a symbol of the rich cultural heritage of the state.
The Governor of the state and many dignitaries attended the
inauguration ceremony. Leaders of various communities as
well as government and non-governmental organizations came
to pay their respects to Guruji. Guruji promised them that
more schools would be started in the remote regions.*

*Satsangs and counseling to help reduce stress and post-
traumatic syndromes have been started in New York, where
our senior teachers are busy.*

*Scientists engaged in research on Sudarshan Kriya are
thrilled by recent findings. Their papers will be published
shortly. At the United Nations in Geneva, the International*

Association for Human Values initiative was adopted, so that official meetings now begin and end with one minute of silence for peace and harmony.

How to Deal With Anxiety

Today many are anxious about how to deal with their anxiety! Here are some of the ways you can manage it:

- Sing, dance and celebrate. The very intention to celebrate will pull you to a more harmonious state.
- Think about what you can do for others rather than about yourself. Get energized with service activities.
- Practice yoga, breathing and meditation.
- Know the impermanence of the world.
- Have faith in and surrender to the Divine. Know that there is a supreme power who loves you, is behind you and accepts you totally. Feeling secure comes with the sense of belongingness.
- Be courageous and invoke the lion within you.
- Have an attitude of sacrifice.
- Remind yourself that you are committed to a greater goal.
- Be unpredictable for a while. Anxiety is always related to some anticipated action so do something completely irrelevant and unpredictable.
- Be ready to face the worst. This will leave you with

stability in the mind.

- Remember a similar situation in the past when you were able to overcome your anxiety.

CHANAKYA: If none of these work, just come and be in the presence of the master! (laughter)

Jai Guru Dev
North American Ashram, Quebec
Canada

News Flash

The International Association for Human Values, based in Geneva, has been chosen as a member of the Swiss Peace Foundation, which is an office of the Swiss Federal Government.

Teacher Training Courses, Phase One and Phase Two, were held at the European Ashram and culminated with Guruji's visit.

The North American Ashram was blushing in fall colors to welcome Guruji.

Several public satsangs and post-traumatic stress relief courses are in progress in the New York/New Jersey area.

Is War Violence or Non-Violence?

Violence and non-violence do not depend on an act but on the intention behind it. The basis of violence is anger, lust, hatred, jealousy, greed, frustration or aggression.

A surgeon cuts open a person's belly, so does a criminal. The action is similar but the surgeon's intention is to save and the criminal's is to destroy. Violence or non-violence is determined by the attitude and not the act.

Even a war can be non-violent if it is devoid of anger, hatred, jealousy or greed and it is for educating someone who cannot be educated in any other way. Even charity can be an act of violence if it takes away self-esteem and inflicts slavery, and a war can be an act of compassion if it helps to establish the right perspective.

Strange but true!

Jai Guru Dev
Bangalore Ashram
India

News Flash

The New York Fire Department has lauded the September 11 contributions of the Art of Living seva team and has sent them a letter of appreciation.

Honey

Let the wind that blows be sweet
Let the oceans flow honey
Let all the herbs and plant kingdom be favorable to us
Let the nights be sweet and let the days be sweet
Let the dust of this planet be sweet to us
Let the heavens and our forefathers be sweet to us
Let all the trees be laden with honey
Let the sun be sweet to us
    and let all the radiations be favorable to us
Let all the animals be sweet to us
Let our food be favorable to us
Let all our thoughts and our speech be sweet like honey

Let our life be pure and divine,
Let it be sweet like honey.

Jai Guru Dev
Bangalore Ashram
India

News Flash

The one who has made our life sweet as honey is in silence!

Weekly Knowledge No. 328
October 29, 2001

Drop Your Intentions

A strong tendency to keep doing something, whether important or unimportant, becomes an impediment to meditation.

"Doing" starts first with an intention and then translates into action. Though intention springs from Being, when it becomes doing it does not let you settle down. All intentions, good or bad, trivial or important, need to be dropped for meditation to happen.

VIJAY: But isn't dropping all intentions itself an intention?

SRI SRI: Yes, but that intention is the last and necessary one. Dropping intentions is not an act. Just the intention to drop them itself serves the purpose. Dropping all intentions even for a moment brings you in touch with your Self and in that instant meditation happens.

While you sit for meditation you have to let the world be the way it is. The repetition of meditation is to habituate your system to stop and start activity at will. The ability to consciously do this is a very precious skill.

Jai Guru Dev
Bangalore Ashram
India

News Flash

During Navaratri there was unmitigated joy from all over the world. Guruji emerged from silence even more radiant, more profound. Many saints visited the Bangalore Ashram during the pujas. A renowned saint from Rishikesh gave daily discourses on the Bhagavatam. Yajñas were performed for the health, happiness and well-being of people all over the world, and to establish peace everywhere. Blessings are always special, but the ecstasy experienced by one and all on Rishi Homa (the last day of Navaratri), as Guruji enthusiastically rushed into the crowds, spraying all his devotees with holy water, was without parallel!

Aishwarya & Madhurya

Usually in places where there is *aishwarya* (lordship) there is no *madhurya* (sweetness), and where there is madhurya there is no aishwarya. Where life has blossomed fully, there is both.

Aishwarya means *ishvaratvaa* — lordship of that which "Is." Wealth, too, is referred to as aishwarya because wealth does command a certain amount of authority.

Can love and authority co-exist? Only in a fully blossomed being is there both lordship and sweetness. There was aishwarya in Sri Rama, but only glimpses of madhurya. In Paraasharam's life there is only lordship, but no madhurya. Buddha manifested more madhurya (the sweetness), and less authority. But Krishna manifested both and so did Jesus. There was lordship when they said, "I am the way!" And there was sweetness in their expressions of prayer and love.

Jai Guru Dev
Bangalore Ashram
India

News Flash

The Art of Living is the only nonprofit organization that was asked to be a part of America Back On Track, a train that is going from Washington to New York, and then on to 20 other cities, as a way of encouraging Americans to return to normal.

Art of Living Courses have started in Uruguay, South America.

The South-East Teachers' Meet ended in immense gratitude and heightened fervor! The Ashram is buzzing with the enthusiasm of more than 200 Teacher Training Course participants!

Volunteer

Who is a volunteer? It is one who comes to help without being asked. One who is self-motivated and inspired becomes a volunteer.

It is possible for a volunteer's inspirational motivation to diminish, which can bring frustration. Usually a volunteer's attitude comes from demand rather than humility, diluting the quality of the service. Another downfall that can happen to volunteers is that they slip away from commitment, thinking there is no "boss"; thinking, "If I like it, I'll do it; if I don't like it, I won't do it!" It is like the steering wheel of a car — if all the tires say they do not need to be steered, then the car cannot move smoothly. If you want to construct a building, you have to accept the authority of the structural engineer, the "boss."

All these problems can only be overcome by being more grounded in spiritual knowledge. A volunteer devoid of a spiritual dimension is utterly weak.

- A volunteer needs to stick to his commitment.
- The integrity of a volunteer comes from his spiritual practices.

- The authority for the volunteer project needs to be acknowledged.
- The strength of a volunteer comes from the challenges he is ready and willing to face.
- A volunteer moves beyond boundaries when he finds he is capable of doing so much more than he ever thought of doing.
- A true volunteer does not expect appreciation or reward. He is thoroughly mistaken if he thinks he is obliging somebody.

A person volunteers because he derives joy from it. That joy itself is the reward, and it is immediate. It does not come on the first of every month in the form of a salary! When a volunteer realizes this, he is filled with gratitude.

When a volunteer waivers from within, his support system is knowledge and good friends.

Jai Guru Dev

Taipei

Taiwan

News Flash

In Delhi, Guruji addressed the U.N. Conference on Volunteerism. Then on to Hong Kong, where he gave an inspiring talk at a beautiful satsang in the packed Grand

Ballroom of the Sheraton Hotel. Today Guruji blessed the inauguration of the Museum of World Religions in Taipei, Taiwan, in the company of the Taiwanese Prime Minister. The founder of the museum, Zen Master Hsin Tao, came and met with Guruji the night before and expressed his gratitude. Tomorrow, Guruji will speak on "The Preservation of Sacred Sites."

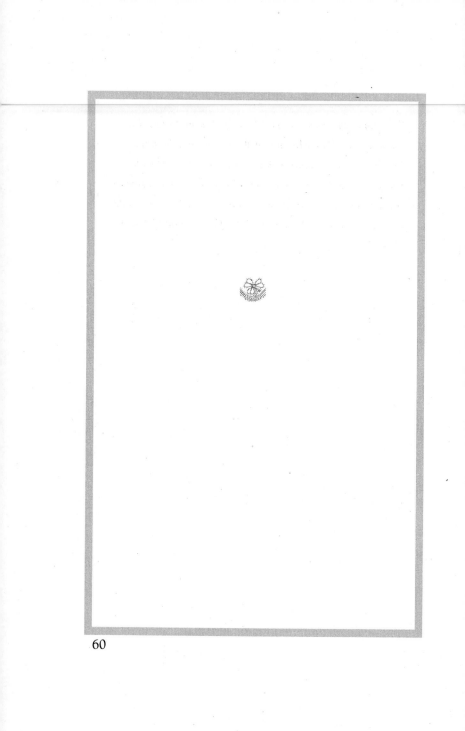

Adulation

Adulation shows the magnanimity of the one who adores, rather than the one who is adored! Adulation is an indicator that the ego has become transparent. The best antidote for ego is adulation.

Adulation works in three ways. If it is for someone else, it is not palatable to an egoistic person. If it is for you, it boosts your ego. If you adore somebody, it dissolves your ego and makes you magnanimous.

GROUP: When Guruji is adulated, EVERYONE adores it! (laughter)

- A desire for adulation is a sign of immaturity.
- Aversion to adulation is small-mindedness.
- Lack of adulation in life is dryness and boredom.
- A healthy mind always likes to adulate, to elevate others.
- An unhealthy mind likes to pull everything down.
- Adulation indicates the trust, enthusiasm and richness in a culture.
- Lack of adulation indicates a self-centered, small-minded, fearful and culturally impoverished society.

Adulation does not sway the one who is great. The test of a person's greatness is that he is not shaken by any amount of adulation. Being indifferent to adulation when it comes to you and being magnanimous when it is to be given is the way of the wise!

Jai Guru Dev
Bangalore Ashram
India

News Flash

Guruji returned to the Bangalore Ashram for a mega Diwali celebration. Twenty years of Ved Vignan Mahavidyapeeth coincided with Dhanvantari (Ayurveda) Day and Dhanteras, the day of wealth! Teacher Training Phase One and Two ended on an enthusiastic high, amid bursting of firecrackers and thousands of jyotis (lit candles). Fifty-seven new teachers have taken off, committed to spreading the knowledge like warriors.

Seva

There are five types of *seva* (service).

- The first type is the seva done when you do not even know that you are doing it. You do not recognize it as seva because it is your very nature — you cannot but do it!
- The second type is the seva which you do because it is needed for that situation.
- You do the third type of seva because it gives you joy.
- The fourth type is done out of your desire for merit — you do seva expecting some benefit in the future.
- And the fifth type is when you do seva just to show off, to improve your image and to gain social or political recognition. Such seva is simply exhausting, while the first type does not bring any tiredness at all!

To improve the quality of your seva, regardless of where you start, you must move up to higher levels of seva.

Jai Guru Dev
Bangalore Ashram
India

News Flash

The Prime Minister of India had an hour-long discussion with Guruji in New Delhi.

It was all celebration in the steel township of Vijyanagar. The highlights of the week were:

- *A mass marriage for the poor where 45 couples were wedded*
- *The 5H Program at work in neighboring villages*
- *Grand satsangs at Bellari and Hospet*
- *A whirlwind tour of the ancient temples of Hampi, Kollur and Udipi, including meetings with the pontiffs of these temple ashrams.*

Weekly Knowledge No. 333
November 29, 2001

Confidence With Humility: the Rarest Combination

One of the rarest character combinations is the co-existence of confidence and humility. Often people who are confident are not humble and people with humility are not confident. Confidence blended with humility is most appreciated by everybody.

QUESTION: How can confidence be developed in one who is humble, and humility in one who is confident?

SRI SRI: First, when you see your life in a bigger context of time and space then you realize your life is nothing. Second, those who are humble need to see that they are unique and dear to the Divine, which brings confidence, and when you realize you are insignificant, that also brings confidence. And third, by having a guru, because he gives you confidence and cultures humility in you. When you have a guru you cannot be arrogant. The weakness in humility and the arrogance in confidence are removed. You are left with confidence and humility!

Jai Guru Dev
Rishikesh
India

News Flash

Guruji had a captive audience while inaugurating the International Convention on Information Technology. He stated that information should be intuitive, communication creative and technology should bring comfort.

In a "flying" visit to Tirupati, Guruji addressed all the Tirupati temple administrators and workers.

The 250 teachers at the Teachers' Refresher Meet in Rishikesh are blissed and blessed!

Dreaming the Impossible

QUESTION: Guruji, how can we control daydreams?

SRI SRI: Dream in the night! (laughter)

What is daydreaming? You have a desire but you do not have the faith that you can achieve your desire — that is what you call daydreaming. You can control daydreaming by having a strong goal and believing in it. Like the scientist who wanted to go to the moon and kept dreaming about it — for him it was the goal of his life but for others it was daydreaming.

Either you drop that it will happen or you believe it will! When you do not know yourself, your potentiality, you have no faith or confidence in your dreams. Once you have faith and confidence in your dreams, they are no longer daydreams!

Jai Guru Dev
New Delhi
India

News Flash

The impossible was made possible at the Youth Training Program (YTP) Meet in Rishikesh. The youths

(Yuvacharyas) are conducting Navchetena Shibirs, satsangs, "creating awareness through cleanliness" campaigns and tree-planting drives, and are busy transforming naxalite-hit villages into "model villages." Within a year 3,000 villages in India were touched and there are now 500 Yuvacharyas. The confidence and commitment of the Yuvacharyas held everyone spellbound as they recounted success tales of alcohol-free, tobacco-free villages, where love and belongingness are being nurtured.

Many terrorists have also been transformed. Immense numbers of legal cases have been withdrawn from courts, with warring factions agreeing to peaceful settlements, especially those involving underprivileged classes. Homes are being given to the needy, Sri Sri Ravishankar Vidya Mandirs opened where schools are not available. Tulsi, neem, genda and other trees are being planted around homes and throughout villages. Two-hundred twenty-four self-help groups have been formed and villagers are encouraged to practice savings. Villagers are celebrating festivals as one big family and human values are increasingly being nurtured.

Over a thousand participants are at the Advanced Course in Rishikesh where they were showered with blessings by a distinguished panel of swamis at the Samapan Samaroh (closing ceremony). The panel also lauded Guruji's worldwide service projects.

Weekly Knowledge No. 335
December 16, 2001

Respect & Ego

There are two types of respect. The first is respect that comes to you because of your position, fame or wealth. This type of respect is impermanent. It can be lost once you lose your wealth or status. The second type of respect comes because of your smile and your virtues, such as honesty, kindness, commitment and patience. This respect no one can take away.

The less you are attached to your virtues, the more self-respect you have. When you get attached to your virtues, you look down upon everybody else and your virtues start diminishing. Non-attachment to virtues brings the highest self-respect.

Often ego is confused with self-esteem. Ego needs the other for comparison, but self-esteem is just confidence in oneself. A gentleman claiming that he is skilled in mathematics or geography is an example of self-esteem. But to say, "I know better than you," is ego.

Ego simply means lack of respect for the Self.

Your ego will often upset you but those with self-esteem are immune to getting upset from external factors. In self-respect everything is a game, winning or losing has no meaning, every step is joy, every move is celebration. In self-esteem you simply realize you have it.

Jai Guru Dev
Bangalore Ashram
India

News Flash

This time all roads did not lead to Rome, but to Florence, where people from all over Italy flocked to meet Guruji. The President of Tuscany, who has also done Art of Living Basic and Advanced Courses, organized the program.

Then Guruji arrived in Lithuania to inspire the assembly of East European teachers and an Advanced Course.

On his return to Bangalore, Guruji blessed 35 Yuvacharyas (youth leaders), who graduated on Sunday and will be taking care of 236 villages spanning four districts under the aegis of the 5H Program.

Maya

What is *maya?*

Maya is that which can be measured. The whole world can be measured, that is why it is Maya. All five elements — earth, water, fire, air and ether — can be measured.

QUESTION: Can space be measured?

SRI SRI: Only in space can things be measured. Space is the first dimension of measurement.

Measurement is always relative and not absolute. For example, if something weighs six kilograms on earth, it will weigh only one kilogram on the moon. The light of the star you see today is not really today's light. It has taken at least four years for the light to reach you! Both size and weight change in air, water and earth. So "measure" is illusive and not dependable. Your bones, skin, body, environment and the five elements can be measured; you can put a value, a quantity, to them. So, the whole world is maya!

All measurements only provide a relative understanding. Einstein's theory of relativity correlates with the *Advaita* (non-dual) philosophy.

But what is not Maya? All that cannot be measured is not Maya. You cannot say one ounce of love, two ounces of peace, and five kilograms of happiness. Can YOU be measured? It is not possible. Your body has weight, but not YOU. Truth cannot be measured, *ananda* (joy) cannot be measured, and beauty cannot be measured. All these are part of consciousness or Ishvara (the Divine), and are called *Mayi*.

Jai Guru Dev
Bangalore Ashram
India

News Flash

A huge satsang in Malleswaram, Bangalore was attended by thousands of people. Guruji's father, Acharya Ratnananda, well known as Pitaji, was felicitated on his 78th birthday.

Letting Go of Control

Many have a problem with letting go of control. This causes anxiety, restlessness and soured relationships.

Wake up and see, are you really in control? What are you in control of? Perhaps a tiny part of your waking state! Isn't that so?

- You are not in control when you are sleeping or dreaming.
- You are not in control of the thoughts and emotions coming to you. You may choose to express them or not, but they come to you without your prior permission!
- Most of the functions of your body are not in your control.

Do you think you are in control of all the events in your life, in the world or in the universe? That is a joke!

When you look at things from this angle you need not be afraid of losing control, because you have none.

Whether you realize it or not, when you let go of your sense of control that is when you truly relax. Your identification of being somebody does not let you totally relax and it limits your domain.

Jai Guru Dev
European Ashram, Bad Antogast
Germany

News Flash
The highlights of Guruji's Chennai visit were a Mahasatsang, a MahaKriya, a Rudra Puja, free medical camps, and more.

This year Guruji deviated from his routine. He was in the Bangalore Ashram to celebrate Christmas where ashramites staged a play of the birth of Christ.

A white blanket of snow covered the Black Forest to welcome Guruji to the European Ashram. The European Teachers' Meet is underway with full zest and vigor.

Memory: a Hindrance & a Blessing

Being forgetful of man's nature is the root cause of all problems and suffering in life. But the very remembrance of one's nature, which is godliness, brings freedom. Here memory is your best friend. The purpose of knowledge is to remind you of your true nature. In the Bhagavad Gita, Arjuna said to Krishna, "I got back my memory. Now I have realized my true nature and will do as you say."

Memory is a blessing and your best friend when it helps you realize your true nature. Memory is a hindrance when it does not let you be free of events, pleasant or unpleasant. Pleasant events create cravings and competition in the mind and do not allow fresh experiences, whereas unpleasant events bias perception and create paranoia. So the memory is both a blessing and a hindrance depending on whether you remember your nature or you are stuck with events in time and space.

Jai Guru Dev
European Ashram, Bad Antogast
Germany

News Flash

The year 2001 was given a fond farewell with an international feast. Participants at the European Ashram held a cultural evening filled with music and dances from several countries represented there. The new year was welcomed with silence and a beautiful meditation with Guruji.

Don't be Perturbed by Foolishness

What really perturbs you? Is it the foolishness that goes on around you?

It is foolish to be perturbed by foolishness. Foolishness cannot overpower or annihilate wisdom nor does foolishness last very long. When you are not well-founded in wisdom then foolishness perturbs you, throws you out of balance. When you create space for foolishness you do not get perturbed by it, rather you will laugh and move on. Otherwise you get hateful or angry, or become stressed by foolish acts.

When you know that truth is eternal and invincible, you accept foolishness as a joke and remain unmoved by it. Those who are averse to foolishness or get irritated by it are members of the Fools Club.

Beware! Do not sign up.

Jai Guru Dev
Austin, Texas
United States

News Flash

A great course in the great state of Texas! January 10th was declared "Sri Sri Ravi Shankar Day" by the Honorable Mayor Garcia of Austin, the capital of Texas. In the past year 310,000 people have benefited from the 5H Program in 7,000 villages.

Glory & Dispassion (Vaibhav & Vairagya)

It is often believed that glory and dispassion are contradictory and cannot co-exist. Glory and luxury without dispassion is a nauseating pomp and show. Such glory does not bring fulfillment for anyone; it is shallow. Alternately, the dispassion that is afraid of glory is weak. True dispassion is oblivious to glory.

The glory that comes with dispassion is something that is true; it is permanent and authentic. When someone chases after glory they are shallow. Movie stars, politicians and religious leaders who try to hold on to their status, to their glory, are certain to lose it. If you run after glory all that you get is misery. When you are dispassionate, glory comes to you.

If you are afraid of glory, that means you are not well-founded in dispassion. In India the *sadhus* run away from glory. They think they will lose their dispassion and get trapped in the web of the world, the circus. The dispassion is so blissful that they get attached to it. They are afraid of losing the dispassion, the centeredness and the bliss that comes along with it. This is weak dispassion.

Dispassion is a state of being and glory is the happening around it. True dispassion can never be lost or overshadowed by glory.

True dispassion is glorious!

Real glory is true dispassion!

Jai Guru Dev
Cascade, Colorado
United States

News Flash

Colorado Springs and Boulder, both in Colorado, had overflowing halls of joy for Guruji's public talks. The students and faculty of Naropa University were ecstatic and inspired finding Guruji with them.

Guruji visited the Garden of the Gods, a sacred site for Native Americans with towering red rock formations. Although the rocks were glorious all eyes were on Guruji! For wherever Guruji goes on this planet, glory follows.

Where Dispassion is Detrimental!

KARTHIK: Is there something we should not be
dispassionate about?

SRI SRI: Myself! (laughter)

Do not put off the fire of longing for the Divine or
for *satsang* with dispassion. There is a little fire in you
that propels you toward knowledge, *sadhana,* devotion
and service but sometimes you use knowledge to put
off that fire. The so-called dispassionate people are
often morose and unenthusiastic. Many times you hear
people saying, "Oh never mind, God is everywhere,
Guruji is in my heart, I can do satsang anywhere. My
seva is my sadhana, so there is no need to meditate.
Anyway I am doing sadhana 24 hours a day. When
God wills he will call me to satsang and Advanced
Courses again!" Such excuses should not be justified
as dispassion.

When you want to do some service, the mind goes,
"Oh it is all *maya* anyway, everything is an illusion. It is
all just happening. Things will happen when the time
comes!"

In this way knowledge gets misused and is quoted

out of context to suit one's convenience or laziness. Using knowledge like this you miss a lot.

In the name of dispassion do not lose that spark of enthusiasm and interest. Keep the fire of longing for the Divine and for service to society alive.

Dispassion here would be detrimental.

Jai Guru Dev
North American Ashram, Quebec
Canada

"Old" Flash

As Guruji spoke on "time," we found the moment, this moment, had passed and the news was already old. The "News" Flash can never be new, so Birjoo decided to call it Old Flash!

Business & Spirituality

Often business is looked down upon by spiritual people, and spirituality is put off as impractical by business people. The ancient people conceived that spirituality is the heart and business is the legs. An individual or a society is incomplete without both these aspects. Business brings material comfort and spirituality brings mental and emotional comfort. Spirituality brings ethics and fair practice to business.

In the body/mind complex, depriving either the body or the mind of comfort means depriving both of them comfort. You cannot talk of spirituality to the poorest of the poor people without taking care of their basic needs. They need to be supported materially. There is no spirituality in the world that is devoid of service and service cannot happen if material needs are ignored. Service cannot happen only through the lips, it needs legs to work.

Every system has its flaws. Capitalism exploits the poor while socialism dampens individual creativity and entrepreneurial spirit. Spirituality is the bridge between socialism and capitalism. Spirituality gives the capitalist the heart to serve and the socialist the spirit to innovate.

Jai Guru Dev
New York City, New York
United States

News Flash

While Guruji attended the World Economic Forum, the Art of Living Foundation was simultaneously being represented at the World Social Forum in Brazil and the U.N. Conference on Sustainable Development in New York.

The Subtle Truth About Virtues

If you observe your behavior, you will notice that you procrastinate when doing something good but hurry when it comes to doing something bad. For example if you are angry, you want to express it immediately.

Do you know why? Because virtues are your very nature and they will never leave you. Your vices are not your nature and they will leave you. Negative tendencies are transient and will leave you if you do not act on them. Frustration and crying cannot stay long, especially with the same intensity. Perhaps you are concerned that your vices will leave you if you do not act on them.

It is wise to postpone acting on vices, for they will not stay, and to act immediately for doing good, otherwise you will continue to postpone doing good for the next few lifetimes. (laughter)

Jai Guru Dev
Bangalore Ashram
India

News Flash

There was an attempt during the World Economic Forum to divide the religious communities into monotheistic and polytheistic. This was given up at Guruji's insistence and harmony finally prevailed. Leaders from all religious communities, including the Archbishop of Canterbury, agreed to drop this draft resolution as Guruji had desired.

An Advanced Course with people from 37 countries is in progress at the Bangalore Ashram.

Humor & Humiliation

Humor is the buffer that saves you from humiliation. If you have a good sense of humor you can never be humiliated, and if you refuse to be humiliated you become invincible. Humor brings people together while humiliation tears them apart. In a society torn with humiliation and insults, humor is like a breath of fresh air. A good sense of humor relieves you from fear and anxiety.

Humor should be coupled with care and concern. Mere humor without care and concern or appropriate action often irritates those who come to you with serious problems.

- Humor can keep spirits high, yet if overdone it leaves a bad taste.
- Humor without wisdom is shallow.
- Humor with wisdom creates an atmosphere of celebration.
- Humor without sensitivity is satire and it returns to you with more problems.
- The wise use humor to bring wisdom and to lighten every situation.

- The intelligent use humor as a shield against humiliation.
- The cruel use humor as a sword to insult others.
- The irresponsible use humor to escape from responsibility.
- The fool takes humor too seriously!
- To make an effort to be humorous is nonsensical.

QUESTION: How does one cultivate a sense of humor?

SRI SRI: Humor is not just words, it is the lightness of your being. Your sense of humor can grow by:

- Being cordial and lighthearted brings out authentic humor, but not by reading and repeating jokes.
- Not taking life too seriously, because you will never come out of it alive! (laughter)
- Having a sense of belongingness with everybody, including those who are not friendly.
- Practicing yoga and meditation.
- Having unshakable faith in the Divine and in the laws of karma.
- Being in the company of those who live in knowledge and who are humorous.
- Having a willingness to be a clown.

Jai Guru Dev
Bangalore Ashram
India

News Flash

On Valentine's Day, jubilant and ecstatic participants of Teacher Training Phase One and Two and the International Advanced Course (more than 700 in all) celebrated with a colorful multilingual cultural program that highlighted Guruji's universal message of love.

After an intensive but blissful course, with nearly eight days of silence and deep meditation, the Advanced Course participants had a surprise picnic with Guruji, visiting an ancient Shiva temple over 5,000 years old. The temple authorities were moved as they recollected the prophecies of two saints which were fulfilled by Guruji's visit.

Love & Truth

Why would someone tell a lie to their close ones or to their beloved?

This is a question often asked by lovers. Love cannot stand untruth, causing relationships to break up when this happens. The answer lies in understanding the paradox of love and truth.

People tell lies just to save and maintain their love. The fear that the truth might damage their love causes lies to be told between husband and wife, boyfriend and girlfriend, parents and children and in other family situations.

In love you feel weak but truth brings strength. Yet why do people prefer love over truth, weakness over strength?

No one wants to sacrifice love. Thus people are ready to give up the truth for their love. Love takes the luster out of truth. Sometimes truth can make love bitter while in love even lies can appear sweet, like Krishna's lies to his mother, Yashoda!

The truth that does not nourish love makes no sense, and the love that cannot withstand the truth is not true love. When one is assured that their love is so strong that the truth can neither break it nor cause bitterness, then the truth prevails and love shines.

With truth there are judgments, but true love is beyond judgments. Thus true love makes you weak and yet it is the greatest strength.

Jai Guru Dev
Bangalore Ashram
India

News Flash

Bliss reigned supreme in the beautiful South Indian state of Kerala. Over a million hearts were stolen by Guruji during his tour of Kerala. Everywhere he went, the script was the same — overflowing stadiums, inspiring and scintillating discourses, deep meditations, tears of gratitude. No one could escape! All the events were highlighted in the media. The Chief Minister of Kerala State and most of his cabinet ministers hosted Guruji at a special function and sought his advice on problems that they were facing.

In Thiruvananthapuram, when the participants opened their eyes after Sudarshan Kriya, they could not see Guruji on the stage, though they could hear his voice. Later they found him sitting on the branch of a tree with a cordless microphone!

An Awkward Situation

Why do you feel awkward? How do you get out of it?

If you have always been the center of attention and are suddenly sidelined, you may feel out of place. Similarly if you have always been on the sidelines and are suddenly pushed to center stage, you may experience restlessness. A very busy person with nothing to do, or a laid-back person who is faced with responsibilities may also experience restlessness. If you are accustomed to ordering others and suddenly have to take orders, or if you usually follow orders and then are made to give them, you may feel out of place. Very often feeling out of place blocks reason and distorts logic.

If the situation you are in is inevitable, tolerate it. If it is avoidable, walk away from it. If you feel that it can expand your abilities, smile through it.

Every awkward situation increases your comfort zone. Every awkward situation is a test for how deep you are in the knowledge.

Love something of an awkward situation. This will increase your comfort zone. When your comfort zone increases, no one will be able to push your buttons and you will become centered and unshakable.

Jai Guru Dev
New Delhi
India

News Flash

From Bangalore to Bihar, the Master has been busy bowling hearts, beautifying interiors and bestowing grace!

From the moment of his tumultuous arrival, Patna opened its heart. The Hathwa Palace brimming over with people, rapturously welcomed Guruji. Evening satsang was at the Beur Jail where the prisoners had a heart-to-heart chat with Guruji. Later, hundreds of students had the benefit of an exclusive session with him. Over 150,000 people experienced his electrifying presence at the Mahasatsang.

The next morning Guruji left for the village of Massauri which has been the target of numerous terrorist attacks. Thousands who have benefited from Navchetena Shibirs (Breath-Water-Sound Workshops) had been preparing for weeks for his visit. Most villagers shared that it was impossible to leave their homes after dusk because of the very volatile and dangerous situation there, but the Shibirs and satsangs had transformed their lives.

Following the Gujarat tragedy, Guruji requested

that everyone observe two minutes of silence on Wednesday, March 6, 2002, at 9 a.m. local time throughout the world for communal peace and harmony and to pay respect to those who were victims of religious intolerance.

The True Yajña

Rage has no ears, nor does it have vision. It only leads to reaction. And reaction leads to regret. Regret causes frustration. Frustration clouds reason. Unreasonable acts provoke rage, starting a vicious cycle.

Self-knowledge and devotion alone can free you from this vicious cycle.

In the fire of knowledge, when rage and revenge are offered, the warmth of the blemishless Self shines forth. This is the true *Yajña*.

Jai Guru Dev
Rishikesh
India

News Flash

Guruji was exceptionally busy this week, meeting various leaders of the Muslim and Hindu communities late into the night to bring peace and harmony and a resolution of the Ayodhya issue. He convinced both the Muslim personal law board and the VHP (Vishva Hindu Parishad – a Hindu society) to come to the negotiating table.

There were remarkably interesting sessions at the AIIMS

(All India Institute of Medical Sciences) symposium on the Science of Breath, some of which Guruji chaired. An international team of doctors presented their research findings to more than 1,000 delegates. A synopsis and videos will be made available by May.

Guruji also went to an impromptu satsang that was organized for him at the Tihar Jail. More than 4,000 inmates who had already gone through the Art of Living Prison Program greeted him enthusiastically. He went among them and showered them with flowers of grace. He noticed that there were some very old women prisoners there who could barely sit or stand by themselves — utterly incapable of committing any crimes. He has made an appeal to the Governor to grant them amnesty.

Your Nature is Shiva

Peace is your nature, yet you remain restless.

Freedom is your nature, yet you remain in bondage.

Happiness is your nature, yet you become miserable
for some reason or another.

Contentment is your nature, yet you continue to reel
in desires.

Benevolence is your nature, yet you do not reach
out.

Going toward your nature is *sadhana*. Sadhana is
becoming what you truly are! Your true nature is
Shiva. And Shiva is peace, infinity, beauty and the non-
dual One.

Ratri means "to take refuge." Shivaratri is taking
refuge in Shiva.

Jai Guru Dev
Rishikesh
India

News Flash

*Guruji was a state guest in Uttaranchal where he was wel-
comed by the Chief Minister. Mr. and Mrs. Mann hosted a*

beautiful satsang in Dehradun.

Shivaratri celebrations in Rishikesh truly took everyone to the peak of bliss and to the silence beyond. Rudra pujas in the morning and evening cast a spell in the air, the chants reverberated through the ashram and stilled hearts and minds. The all-night satsang included thousands, and it ended with an early morning Sudarshan Kriya with the master.

Praise the Fools

Praising the fool is beneficial to society!

A fool when pleased might stop doing harm and start doing good work. In this sense it is wise to praise a fool; it helps to motivate him. So your praise is meaningful when it is directed toward a fool.

A wise man by his very nature will continue doing good work because his attitude does not depend on someone's praise or blame. So it serves no purpose to praise a wise man because your praise will have no impact on him.

There are three types of people — the wise, the crooked and the immature. The wise man continues doing good work even if he is scolded or praised. Crooked people need to be praised to get them to do good work. And from time to time the immature person needs to be both praised and scolded for them to do something good.

Jai Guru Dev
Rishikesh
India

News Flash

A close associate of Osama Bin Laden, Mohammad Afroz, who is currently in the high security Bombay prison, was involved in the plan to blow up a London airport. He took the Art of Living Prison Program and was totally transformed. He wrote that he wished that all Al Qaeda members would do the course that brought forth such a transformation in him. His desire is to become an Art of Living teacher and bring peace and harmony to people!

At the same time Reverend Sri Shiva Muniji Maharaj, a proponent of non-violence (ahimsa) and the head of the Jain religion, was on the Advanced Course and proclaimed the fulfillment of the Jain religion from what he found in the Art of Living.

The participants on the third Advanced Course are soaking in bliss on the banks of the Ganges River.

What Makes a Real Holiday

Rest and happiness make a real holiday. Often people go on a holiday and they come back tired and tanned, but needing a few more days to recuperate! A real holiday is that which energizes you and does not wear you out.

Nothing energizes you like wisdom, so remember:

- Doubts and complaints are impediments to rest.
- The moment you set out on your holiday, know that it has begun. Often people expect to find a pinnacle of happiness. Enjoy every moment of the journey as children do, do not wait for the destination.
- If you cannot be happy in one place, you cannot be happy in any other place. If you do not know how to row one boat, you will not be able to row any other boat.
- To get maximum satisfaction out of your holiday you need to do something creative and to engage in seva.
- Do not ever forget to make meditation and prayer a

part of your holiday.

If your days are holy, then every day is a holiday!

Jai Guru Dev
New Delhi
India

News Flash

Holi, the festival of colors, was celebrated with enthusiasm and jubilation. Over 5,000 people were awash with blessings, bliss and myriad hues of happiness. Satsang continued through the day as Guruji showered colors and love on people's lives.

On to Delhi, where Guruji addressed the Chambers of Commerce and several top Muslim leaders. Later Guruji visited the Hazrat Nizamuddin Dargah Sharief and was given a reception at the Fatehpuri Masjid.

Wake Up & Slow Down

Often you are in a rush in life. When you are in a rush,
you are unable to properly perceive things. This takes
the charm, thrill and beauty from your life. You can
never be close to the truth when you are in a rush
because your perception, observation and expression
become distorted.

The rush to enjoy robs the joy from life and only
denies the happiness and freedom of here and now.
Often you do not even know why you are in a hurry.
It almost becomes a biological phenomenon to be in a
rush. Wake up and become aware of the rush in you!

ANNE FARROW: Wake up and slow down! (laughter)

It is ridiculous to be in a rush to slow down. Just
being aware of the rush itself will take care of it.
Slowing down does not mean procrastinating or being
lethargic, though it is easy to be at the extremes of
either rushing or lethargy. Rushing is caused by feverishness, and feverishness arises out of deficiency, a
need to achieve; whereas dynamism is an expression of
fulfillment.

The golden rule is to be awake, and when you are

awake you cannot help but be dynamic.

Right now realize that you are awake and cool.

Jai Guru Dev
Gangtok, Sikkim
India

News Flash

Guruji was a state guest in Arunachal Pradesh where he addressed the ministers and NGO's, he inaugurated the Art of Living International School, and he addressed the intellectuals at the Arunachal Pradesh University in the scenic Rono Hills. On the way to a satsang in Itanagar, Guruji visited the local Nyishi tribe who pray to the sun god.

On to Guwahati, Assam, where the heavens held their rain for a satsang and live Sudarshan Kriya attended by thousands of people. Guruji inaugurated a model village near Tezpur and laid a foundation stone for a new technical school and ashram on the banks of the Brahmaputra River.

Thousands attended a satsang in Siliguri, West Bengal, as Guruji traveled northward to Sikkim.

Communism & Spirituality

Communism has three goals: To check the greed of feudal and capitalistic societies; to halt the fanaticism and fundamentalism of religious communities; and to care for and share resources with the needy.

Only spirituality brings fulfillment to communism. Only spirituality checks greed and opens the hearts of the rich to help the needy. Only spirituality stops the fanaticism and fundamentalism of religious groups and creates a sense of belongingness with the whole world. Only spirituality cultures the tendency to care and share. Only spirituality brings about open-mindedness and a progressive attitude.

Communism cannot fulfill its goals without spirituality. It is impossible and time has proved it. Spirituality nourishes communism.

Knowledge Nibble!

QUESTION: If you have a guru do you need luck?

SRI SRI: You need luck to have a guru! (laughter)

Jai Guru Dev
Bangalore Ashram
India

News Flash

Guruji was in Sikkim for a huge satsang. He later visited the Rumtek Monastery where he was given a traditional Buddhist welcome. Thousands thronged the largest stadium in Kolkata for a rousing satsang and a deep rejuvenating meditation with Guruji.

For the first time, 700 people boarded the Enlightenment Express from Mumbai to Bangalore for a wonderful Advanced Course with Guruji.

Was Buddha an Atheist?

A pure atheist is impossible to find. An atheist is one who does not believe in anything that is not concrete and tangible, but life is not all concrete and tangible, nor is this universe. Whether it is business, science or art, all involve a certain amount of guesswork, assumptions, imagination and intuition. All of them are ethereal in nature and are not tangible.

The moment an atheist accepts, even remotely, a field that is unexplainable, he ceases to be an atheist. An intelligent person cannot rule out the mysteries in life and the universe, and hence cannot honestly be an atheist! The so-called atheists are perhaps only denouncing certain concepts of God.

QUESTION: Was Buddha an atheist?

SRI SRI: No, in one sense, because he professed emptiness, which is very hard for an atheist to accept. And yes, in another sense, because he did not profess concepts of God.

JIM: An atheist believes only what he can see, but Buddha said all that you see is not real.

SRI SRI: If only all present-day atheists could
be Buddhas.

Jai Guru Dev
Bangalore Ashram
India

The Strength of Commitment

QUESTION: Why is it easier for some of us to commit to our own welfare rather than that of others?

SRI SRI: Because you do not know that whatever you are committed to brings you strength.

If you are committed to your family then your family supports you. If you are committed to your society, you enjoy the support of society. If you are committed to God, God gives you strength. If you are committed to truth, truth brings you strength.

Often people are not aware of this and that is why they are hesitant to commit to a greater cause. There is also a fear that commitment would weaken people or take away their freedom. Your commitment to a cause is bound to bring you comfort in the long run.

Commitment in life grows toward a higher cause. The higher the commitment, the greater is the good for all.

NOAH: Why don't we take any vows in the Art of Living?

SRI SRI: When the path is charming, commitment is effortless and is part of your nature.

MIKEY: In the Art of Living we don't take vows, we have wows! (laughter)

Jai Guru Dev
Boston, Massachusetts
United States

News Flash

Guruji's visit to Saarbruken and Stutgaart in Germany was extensively covered by the media. Three more universities in Berlin have made the Art of Living Course a part of their curriculum, for a total of five universities officially offering the course.

Hundreds of participants were graced by Guruji's presence at the one-day Advanced Course in New Jersey. Following an intimate satsang in New York, Guruji gave a surprise public talk in Washington, D.C.

Hundreds of students were inspired by Guruji's talk in Amherst and Boston.

Weekly Knowledge No. 355
May 11, 2001

Two Types of Knowledge

There are two types of knowledge. The first one is
pure knowledge and the second one is applied knowledge. Applied knowledge may benefit you directly and
immediately, but pure knowledge benefits you indi-
rectly and in the long run.

If there are some things that you have studied or
understood that you are unable to put into practice, do
not get disheartened. Sometime in the future, if you
do not discard the knowledge you have as impractical,
it will be of use to you.

Often people discard pure knowledge for its lack of
immediate application. In fact these two types of
knowledge complement each other. Applied knowledge without pure knowledge remains weak. And pure
knowledge without application will remain unfulfilled.

Do not discard or label the knowledge as impractical, and do not label yourself as weak or unworthy
because you are unable to apply the knowledge in your
day-to-day life.

Sometimes when you are alone in nature, silent,
taking a walk, looking at the sand on the beach, a

bird in the sky, or while meditating — suddenly the knowledge will emerge and you will recognize the knowledge dawning in your life.

Jai Guru Dev
Palo Alto, California
United States

News Flash

Guruji went to Venice, Italy, where he inaugurated the international conference entitled "World Peace Through Prayer and Meditation."

In Switzerland, Art of Living Courses will be offered to high school teachers as part of their continuing education.

Mera Lee Goldman, the Mayor of Beverly Hills, California, officially proclaimed May 9, 2002, to be "His Holiness Sri Sri Ravi Shankar Day." On May 6, the Mayor of Los Angeles, California, James K. Hahn, formally recognized the activities of the Art of Living Foundation for "outstanding efforts and accomplishments which have been of great benefit to the City of Los Angeles."

An Advanced Course is being held now in the San Francisco Bay area.

Friendship for a Cause

Examine your friendships for their cause. Here are the reasons:

- You make friends because you have common enemies. Fear or a threat to survival brings people together.
- You make friends because you have common problems such as sickness or job dissatisfaction.
- People get together and become friends because they have common interests. Examples are business people or professionals such as doctors, architects or social workers.
- You make friends because of common tastes. Examples of this are common interests in sports, movies, music and hobbies.
- People become friends with those for whom they have compassion or provide service.
- People become friends merely because of a long-term acquaintance.

Brave are those who nurture friendships for only friendship's sake. Such friendships will never die nor become soured for they are born out of one's friendly

nature. Only through wisdom is one friendly by
nature.

Jai Guru Dev
Jakarta, Java
Indonesia

News Flash

*On Guruji's birthday, May 13, seva projects and satsangs
were held all over the world. Thousands of poor and needy
were fed and received clothes.*

*From San Jose, Guruji traveled to Bali with a brief
stopover in Japan. In Bali an Advanced Course was held for
South East Asia and Australia. Then Guruji went to
Yogjakarta, Indonesia, to visit one of the seven wonders of the
world. After satsangs in Jakarta and Singapore, Guruji will
leave for Bangalore.*

Three Types of Dispassion

There are three types of dispassion:

- The first type is the dispassion that arises when you realize the misery in the world and you fear misery. The events in life — the pain and suffering you experience or see — bring dispassion.
- The second type of dispassion is born out of your desire to achieve something higher. Some consider dispassion as a path to enlightenment by renouncing something here to gain something out there. They engage in austerities and take vows to have a better place in heaven.
- The third type of dispassion comes from wisdom or knowledge. A broader understanding of the transient nature of things cultures a state of non-attachment to events, objects, people or situations which lets you remain calm and unperturbed.

Divine love does not let dispassion manifest. The attainment of love brings such bliss and such intoxication that it not only takes away your passion, but dispassion as well.

This is the problem with many Art of Living

members. They feel they have attained the highest and remain blissed out!

Jai Guru Dev
Jakarta, Java
Indonesia

Faith & Alertness

Faith and alertness appear to be completely opposite in nature. When you are alert there usually is no faith, and you feel restless and insecure. When you have faith your mind is secure and in a restful state, and you are not alert.

There are three types of faith:

- *Tamasic* faith is caused by dullness. An example is when you do not want to take responsibility or action and you say, "Oh, it doesn't matter, God will take care of all these things!" (laughter)

- *Rajasic* faith is brought on by an intense compulsion of desires and ambition. The ambition keeps your faith alive.

- *Satvic* faith is innocent and is born out of fullness of consciousness.

Faith and alertness, though apparently opposite in nature, are actually complementary to each other. In the absence of faith there can be no growth, and without alertness there can be no correct understanding. Faith can make you complacent while alertness makes you tense. If there is no faith, there is fear. And when there is no alertness you cannot perceive or express properly, so a combination of both is essential.

In *gyana* (a state of wisdom) there is alertness without tension and faith without complacency. The purpose of education should be to remove the element of dullness from faith and the element of fear from alertness. This is a unique and rare combination. If you have faith and alertness at the same time, then you will become a true *gyani* (wise one).

Jai Guru Dev
Bangalore
India

News Flash

The YLTP (Youth Leadership Training Program) trainer's meeting concluded last week with great enthusiasm and celebration.

A huge contingent from Kerala came to the Bangalore Ashram for an Advanced Course with Guruji.

A teacher training program is in progress for those who will be teaching in the Sri Sri Ravishankar Vidya Mandir schools all over the country.

Enthusiasm & Dispassion

What is enthusiasm? Enthusiasm means to be connected to God within. When you are with your source, you can only be enthusiastic, and you cannot be but enthusiastic when your mind is totally in the present moment. Apathy is when you are away from the source of life.

You should know that dispassion is not apathy; it is simply a broader perspective of reality. Dispassion is moving toward the source. Dispassion simply means the way back home. It is the journey toward the source, which is a reservoir of enthusiasm.

When dispassion and enthusiasm co-exist, that is the secret of perennial enthusiasm and profound dispassion. Though they appear to be opposite, they are actually complementary.

Jai Guru Dev
Washington, D.C.
United States

News Flash

An 11th-century temple rose from ruins in Guruji's birthplace of Thayagasamudram, thanks to the sole effort of one of our Art of Living teachers, Setu Mamy. Though about 80 years old, her enthusiasm was that of a teenager. Single-handedly she overcame all hurdles to bring this temple back to life. It was a grand celebration in the village. Guruji promised to build homes for needy people there.

Guru Tidbits

What to do if your commitment is boring?
Commitment has value when things are not so
charming. When things are interesting you do not
need commitment at all. You never say you are committed to doing something that is very interesting or
charming.

Learning.
Learning is inevitable. By doing things right you
learn, and by doing things wrong you also learn. From
every situation, from everybody, you learn either what
to do or what not to do. Either by mistakes or by
doing things correctly, you cannot but learn. Learning
is inevitable.

It is only when you sleep that you do not learn. And
if you are asleep in your life, there is neither pain nor
pleasure nor learning. Most people are in such deep
slumber. That is why many people do not even make
an effort to get out of their pain.

QUESTION: How do I improve my patience?

SRI SRI: Can I tell you next year? (laughter)

QUESTION: How do I improve my memory?

SRI SRI: Ask me this question later. (laughter)

Jai Guru Dev
Washington, D.C.
United States

News Flash

Guruji went to Kumbakonam where there was a huge satsang of several hundred thousand in the biggest temple city of Tamil Nadu.

Then on to Heidelberg and Berlin in Germany where people came in large numbers to attend talks and satsangs. While there, he was received at the Indian Embassy and met with several senators from the German Congress.

Nigraha, Agraha, Satyagraha & Duraagraha

Nigraha means control. *Agraha* means insistence. *Satyagraha* means steadfast determination. *Duraagraha* means blind adamancy, reckless stubbornness.

These four allow you to progress when practiced for just a limited period of time and will give limited results, positive or negative. But if practiced for a long period of time, they will eat away the potential of life. You have to transcend all four to attain peace.

Freedom is when you transcend all four. They are inevitable to streamline life but you need to transcend them to be free.

EXERCISE: Give your own examples and discuss nigraha, agraha, satyagraha and duraagraha.

Jai Guru Dev
Washington, D.C.
United States

News Flash

Guruji's North American tour began in Chicago, where he was the keynote speaker at the meeting of the American Association of Physicians of Indian Origin. He also received a letter of appreciation from the United States Congress and one from Mayor Daley of Chicago. June 28 was declared "His Holiness Sri Sri Ravi Shankar Day" in Chicago.

Wake Up & Transcend

The foolish one uses spiritual power to gain material comfort.

An intelligent one uses the material world to rise high in the spirit.

When you transcend the intellect you allow yourself to be used by the spirit.

One who is awake neither uses anything nor loses anything.

Become intelligent, transcend and wake up.

Jai Guru Dev
Undisclosed
United States

News Flash

Guruji gave the inaugural address at the American Telugu Association Conference in Dallas on July 5. His inspiring words left the audience wanting more. A group of hecklers tried to stop Guruji's public talk but mysteriously dispersed as his car approached. He charmed the Texas crowd with his humor and knowledge.

The first ever North American YLTP (Youth Leadership

Training Program) took place in Brownsville, Texas. These college students and their friends are now Breath-Water-Sound teachers and are traveling in Belize and Mexico offering this fantastic course to people in impoverished villages and barrios.

Art of Living Foundation
Programs & Courses

The Art of Living Foundation

THE ART OF LIVING FOUNDATION (www.artofliving.org)
is devoted to making life a celebration. A nonprofit educational organization run by volunteers, it offers programs for self-development and spiritual growth that
allow busy people to take maximum advantage
of Sri Sri's multidimensional teachings. The Foundation is
recognized as an official Non-Governmental
Organization (NGO) of the United Nations, developing
and sponsoring service projects worldwide, including
programs for people living with HIV and cancer, rehabil-
itative training for prisoners, and vocational training for
rural people.

The Foundation's CARE FOR CHILDREN "Dollar-a-Day"
program (www.careforchildren.org) provides children
with food, clothing and education.

Founded in 1981, and accredited as a charitable nonprofit institution, VED VIGNAN MAHAVIDYAPEETH (Institute
of Vedic Science) provides many essential educational and
medical services. The only source of free education in the
rural area surrounding Bangalore, India, this top-rated

Institute serves boys and girls from 22 villages. All services are administered at no charge to each child through funding from supporting individuals and groups.

THE 5-H PROGRAM (www.5H.org) is a joint effort of the Art of Living Foundation in India and the International Association for Human Values (www.IAHV.org). The 5-H Program offers social and community development projects with a focus on Health, Hygiene, Homes, Harmony in diversity, and Human values. This unique and comprehensive approach involves training youths to become community leaders. IAHV's Homes for Change program is building homes, wells, and septic systems for poor families in developing countries.

THE ART OF LIVING COURSE is the cornerstone of Sri Sri's wisdom. The 16–18-hour program is usually offered over six days and has uplifted the lives of more than one million people worldwide. Breath contains the secret of life and is a link to vital life energy, or prana. Low prana causes depression, lethargy, dullness and poor enthusiasm. A mind and body charged with prana is alert, energetic and happy. Specific breathing techniques taught on the course revitalize and invigorate both physical and emotional well-being. Among these techniques is a powerful process called *Sudarshan Kriya,* which fully oxygenates the cells, recharging them with new energy and life, washing away negative emotions stored as toxins in the body. Tension, anger, anxiety, depression and lethargy are released and forgotten. The mind is left calm and centered, with a clearer vision of the world, relationships and and our own self. The course also includes processes and deep insights into the nature of life and happiness. For a schedule of courses near you, contact one of the Art of Living Centers listed on page 137.

ADVANCED COURSES are specially designed for those who have completed the Art of Living Course. These retreats, spent partially in silence, provide a profound opportunity to explore the depths of your own inner silence through deep meditation, service and enjoyable processes. Each evening ends with a celebration of singing, dancing and astounding wisdom. You leave feeling renewed emotionally and elevated spiritually, with a dynamism for greater success in all your activities. Some Advanced Courses are offered in Sri Sri's presence, which is the experience of a lifetime.

SAHAJ SAMADHI MEDITATION is another gift from Sri Sri. Not one of us lacks spiritual depth. The peace and happiness we seek in the world is already within us, but masked by stress and strain. Sahaj Samadhi Meditation provides a rest much deeper than sleep, releasing deep-rooted stresses and energizing our nervous systems. Like awakening renewed on a sunny morning, your outlook on life becomes more positive. Stress drops off, the chattering mind becomes serene and creative, aging slows and you rediscover the unshakable contentment of your inner Self. Sahaj Samadhi Meditation is easy to learn and practice. With simple guidance, anyone can meditate. Personal instruction is offered at Art of Living Centers worldwide.

Our course for children and teens, ART EXCEL (All 'Round Training In Excellence) includes a rich human values component that cultures students in such values as acceptance of others, empathy, respect, trust and selfless giving. Students are challenged to go beyond their limited perspectives to consider the world at large with all its diversity. The true measure of success is a happy, healthy, well-adjusted child who is able to deal effectively with life's challenges. Find out more at www.artexcel.info.

To learn more about the Art of Living Foundation and its programs, visit www.artofliving.org.

Art of Living Bookstore

Sri Sri's teachings are available in the form of books, videotapes, DVD's, audiotapes and CD's. Titles include *God Loves Fun, Celebrating Silence, The Path of Love, Compassion and Trust, The Purpose of Life, The Ultimate Relationship, Om Shanti Shanti Shanti, the Yoga Sutras of Patanjali, A Gift of Silence* (guided meditations by Sri Sri on CD), and other volumes of *An Intimate Note to the Sincere Seeker.*

For a catalog of products and to order, contact:

VYAKTI VIKAS KENDRA • INDIA
Tel. 91-80-6645106
Fax: 91-80-8432832
E-mail: vvkpress@vsnl.com

ART OF LIVING BOOKSTORE • USA
Tel. 877-477-4774 (U.S.A.) or 641-472-9892
Fax: 641-472-0671
E-mail: bookstore@artofliving.org
www.bookstore.artofliving.org

ART OF LIVING BOOKS & TAPES • EUROPE
Tel. +49-7804-9109223
Fax: 49-7804-910924
E-mail: IntAOLEurope.BooksandTapes@t-online.de

Worldwide Art of Living Centers

The Art of Living Foundation is in more than 130 countries. For information about courses and programs near you, contact one of the centers below, or visit www.artofliving.org.

AFRICA
Art of Living
Hema & Rajaraman
P.O. Box 1213
Peba Close Plot 5612
Gaborone, Botswana
Tel. 26-735-2175
aolbot@global.co.za

CANADA
Art of Living Foundation
P.O. Box 170
13 Infinity Rd.
Saint-Mathieu-du-Parc
Quebec G0X 1N0
Canada
Tel. 819-532-3328
artofliving.northamerica@sympatico.ca

EUROPE
Akademie Bad Antogast
Bad Antogast 1
77728 Oppenau
Germany
Tel. 49-7804-910-923
Artofliving.Germany@t-online.de

INDIA
Vyakti Vikas Kendra, India
No. 19, 39th A Cross,
11th Main
4th T Block, Jayanagar
Bangalore 560041, India
Tel. 91-80-6645106
vvm@vsnl.com

UNITED STATES
Art of Living Foundation
P.O. Box 50003
Santa Barbara, CA 93150
Tel. 805-564-1002
U.S. toll-free: 877-399-1008
info@artofliving.org

AUSTRALIA
Canberra :
Katie Schmitz and Rob Bourke
27, Ironside St. Weston ACT 2611
Ph : 61-2-6287-4004
Email : katierob@orac.net.au

Sydney :
Ivan and Sarah Brownrigg
P.O. Box : 1976 Nth Sydney 2059
Ph. : +61(0) 2 9959 5226
Fax : +61(0) 2 9922 2690
Email : sydney@artofliving.org.au
Website : www.artofliving.org.au

NEW ZEALAND
Simin and Marcus Williams
P.O. Box 997, Gisborne
Tel. : 06-868-8002
Fax : 06-868-8042
Email : artofliving@xtra.co.nz

RUSSIA
Valentin Tongaluk
Deputatskaya Street 43/5-8 664023
Irkutsk 664023
Tel. : (3952) 530540
Email : tonga@irk.ru

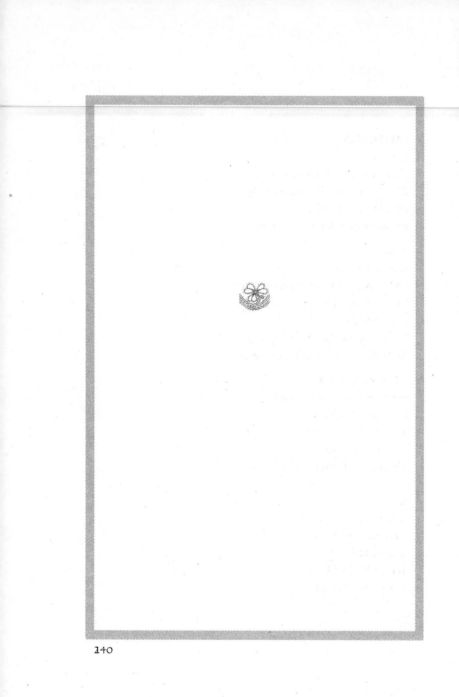